Messages of

for **Advent** and
Christmas 2020

Messages of

Joy

for **Advent** and **Christmas 2020**

3-MINUTE DEVOTIONS

MICHAEL WHITE and **TOM CORCORAN**

Ave Maria Press AVE Notre Dame, Indiana

Founded in 1865, Ave Maria Press is a ministry of the United States Province of Holy Cross.

www.avemariapress.com

Paperback: ISBN-13 978-1-64680-003-2

E-book: ISBN-13 978-1-64680-004-9

Cover and text design by Samantha Watson.

Printed and bound in the United States of America.

Introduction

Christmas is the season of giving. While the marketing and advertising that surround gift-giving can certainly get out of hand, our culture still implicitly understands that Christmas is all about giving. And the giving begins with God.

God is a giver, and everything is a gift. He has given us the earth. He has given us our talents and abilities, our friends and families, our opportunities, our possessions, and everything else we have besides. God is a giver. God is generous. At Christmas we celebrate that God the Father gave us his best by giving us his Son.

John 3:16 says, "For God so loved the world he *gave* his only Son" (emphasis added). And then the Son loves us so much he gives his life for us that we might have life. God loves, so God gives.

Since God is a generous giver, growing as followers of Christ means growing in generosity. If we are becoming more like Christ, then we will be generous as he is generous. And while generosity includes financial giving, it is much wider than that. Nearly every moment of every day we have an opportunity to give something to someone else: our time, our insight, our encouragement, a smile, or credit for success.

It is tempting for us to think of generosity and giving as a label for larger-than-life heroes such as Mother Teresa, but giving doesn't necessarily require extraordinary acts of service. It simply involves focusing on others rather than on ourselves. When we look to the end of our lives we want to be remembered as people who gave. No one is ever honored for what they received or took from others. People who are honored and remembered fondly are remembered for their contributions to others.

But we all face obstacles to growing in generosity. The first is simply our own selfishness. As a result of original sin, we tend to think of ourselves first and at the exclusion of others. This is why we have to teach children to share. We can become so consumed with our own problems and feelings that we fail to notice the people around us.

A second obstacle that flows from the first is that we fear we won't have enough. We think, *If I give my money or resources then I won't have enough for me and my family. If I share a contact to help you, then that contact will be less likely to help me. If I give my time to you, I won't have enough time to get done what I need to get done.* We often think of life as a zero-sum game in which generosity decreases our resources.

A third obstacle we face is the fear of being taken advantage of. We have all been duped by dishonest people, and it doesn't feel good. It actually hurts our hearts and can turn us off giving entirely.

While these obstacles are real, they are not insurmountable. They can be overcome through practicing prayer. *Practicing prayer* means not only prayer itself but putting into action what we discover in prayer. As we prayerfully come before

God, the Holy Spirit will prompt us to take action in our lives. The following pages are intended to aid you in that conversation.

In Advent, more than any other time of year, we are inclined to give to others what we have been given. That's the spirit of Christmas, and our job is to give in to that temptation.

The Christmas season reminds us that God treats us generously. God gave us his Son. But when we unwrap Christmas, we discover a generous and giving God who keeps on giving as an example for us to follow. That's the message of joy the season brings.

Fr. Michael and Tom

FIRST WEEK

OF ADVENT

Sunday, November 29

During the Christmas season, we are continually bombarded by advertisements about finding the perfect gift. While it certainly can get out of hand, our culture correctly understands that Christmas is all about giving.

God is a giver. A generous giver. In fact, everything we own and are—our talents, our possessions, our opportunities, etc.—belong to him. As John 3:16 tells us: "For God so loved the world that he *gave* his only Son" (emphasis added).

....

Today, pray for the insight to see all the gifts God has given you. Think about where and when and how you are a giver. Sometimes it doesn't take much to become a giver and become more like Christ. It can be a smile, a kind word, an encouragement or wisdom you share, or perhaps a helping hand. Pray that you become an ever more generous giver this last month of the year.

Monday, November 30

> I have never wanted anyone's silver or gold or clothing. You know well that these very hands have served my needs and my companions. In every way I have shown you that by hard work of that sort we must help the weak, and keep in mind the words of the Lord Jesus who himself said, "It is more blessed to give than to receive."
>
> —Acts 20:33–35

With these words, St. Paul says goodbye to the presbyters from Ephesus and continues his journey. Paul reminds them that there is more blessing and happiness in giving than in receiving. The Bible uses the word *believe* 275 times, the word *pray* 371 times, and the word *love* 714 times. But it uses the word *give* or *giving* 2,162 times. This is how much God values giving.

Giving brings joy. On the other hand, the root word of *miserable* is *miser*. If I do not share, it makes me feel miserable. The more I hold onto things that I possess, the less I enjoy them. Charles Dickens's Ebenezer Scrooge is the archetype of the miser ("Darkness was cheap, and Scrooge liked it"), but thanks to the three ghosts and his nephew, he finally gives in to the spirit of Christmas: "I am as light as a feather, I am as happy as an angel, I am as merry as a schoolboy. I am as giddy as a drunken man. A merry Christmas to everybody! A happy New Year to all the world!"

....

Today, pray for the grace to see the joy of generosity and giving.

Tuesday, December 1

One person is lavish yet grows still richer;
    another is too sparing, yet is the poorer.
Whoever confers benefits will be amply enriched,
    and whoever refreshes others will be
    refreshed.

                 —Proverbs 11:24–25

This is the great paradox of giving: The more you give, the more you have. People are not honored for what they have received or even earned but rather for what they have given to others, for what they have given away.

Studies show that people who volunteer their time, donate money, and are emotionally available and giving in relationships are usually happier and less often depressed. However, being generous demands a lot of practice, and we need to overcome certain obstacles. Very often, we are so occupied with ourselves that we do not even think about others. Proverbs tells us it is in our own best interest not to be solely concerned with ourselves and our own wants and needs.

....

Pray today for the grace to be generous and to identify opportunities to be generous.

Wednesday, December 2

Give and gifts will be given to you; a good measure, packed together, shaken down, and overflowing, will be poured into your lap. For the measure with which you measure will in return be measured out to you.

—Luke 6:38

Jesus teaches that when we give, we open ourselves up to receive even more. The image Jesus uses here is of someone going to a marketplace to buy grain. They would carry the grain back home in their cloak. The grain they receive is so much that the cloak can no longer contain the grain but instead is overflowing.

When we give to others, God pours blessings into our lives that we cannot contain. Some we will see in this life, others in the next. We cannot outgive God. When we are generous with our time, talent, and treasure, we open up ourselves to receive greater blessings in return.

....

Pray to have the mindset of Jesus, who made mercy and generosity a priority.

Thursday, December 3

And the king will say to them in reply, "Amen, I say to you, whatever you did for one of these least brothers of mine, you did for me."

—Matthew 25:40

In this gospel reading, Christ, the king, speaks of the seven corporal acts of mercy and says that whatever we have given to the least of our brothers and sisters, we have given to him. So if we have given food to the hungry and drink to the thirsty, welcomed the strangers, clothed the naked, visited the sick and imprisoned, and buried the dead, we have done something for him. We have opportunities to do these both literally and figuratively. In addition to those who suffer from physical hunger and thirst, there are also people we see every day who hunger and thirst for encouragement, for a smile, for solace, or for wisdom and insight.

....

Be on the lookout to give what you have to the people around you. Ask God to help you notice three opportunities to give to people in need.

Friday, December 4

Iron is sharpened by iron;
   one person sharpens another.
                              —Proverbs 27:17

Proverbs speaks about how people sharpen each other by using a play on words in the original Hebrew: iron sharpens the "face" (the Hebrew word *panim* here means "surface" or "edge") of iron, and a person sharpens the "face" (the Hebrew word *panim* here means "face" or "words") of another. Humans learn and grow in wisdom as they interact and talk with each other. This is God's vision for his children: that they would be constantly giving to one another.

In addition to the seven corporal acts of mercy, there are also the seven spiritual acts of mercy that show specific ways to give to others: instruct the uninformed, counsel the doubtful, be patient with those who wrong us, forgive offenses, correct the sinner, comfort the afflicted, and pray for the living and the dead. These acts are both how we sharpen and give to each other.

....

Look at the seven corporal acts of mercy. Pray for the strength and courage to seize the next opportunities to live them.

Saturday, December 5

Daniel 3:82–87

Give glory and eternal praise to him.
"You sons of men, bless the Lord;
     praise and exalt him above all forever."
Give glory and eternal praise to him.
"O Israel, bless the Lord;
     praise and exalt him above all forever."
Give glory and eternal praise to him.
"Priests of the Lord, bless the Lord;
     praise and exalt him above all forever."
Give glory and eternal praise to him.
"Servants of the Lord, bless the Lord;
     praise and exalt him above all forever."
Give glory and eternal praise to him.
"Spirits and souls of the just, bless the Lord;
     praise and exalt him above all forever."
Give glory and eternal praise to him.
"Holy men of humble heart, bless the Lord;
     praise and exalt him above all forever."
Give glory and eternal praise to him.

Second Week

OF ADVENT

Sunday, December 6

When you get to the core of Christmas, it is all about giving. This is why we call it the season of giving. At Christmas God gave us his greatest gift. John 3:16 tells us, "God so loved the world, he gave his only Son." God loves so God gives. God gives his Son, and then Jesus gives his life that we might have life.

God gives, and so if we are growing to be more like him, we will grow in our giving and generosity. While this includes giving financially, being a generous person is not just about giving money but also giving anything we have to others. We can be generous by giving our time, sharing a contact, or offering encouragement or wisdom to others.

Giving makes us more like God, and we benefit from it as well. Jesus said, "It is more blessed to give than to receive" (Acts 20:35). And in the end it is the givers and generous people who will inherit eternal life.

This week, look at giving the gift of presence. One of the most frequent promises God makes to his people and to the heroes of the Bible is "I will be with you." The story of the Bible isn't about people's search for God, but God's desire to be with his people.

....

Thank God today that he wants to be with you and for you to know his presence.

Monday, December 7

You, LORD, are our father,
    our redeemer you are named from of old.
Why do you make us wander, LORD, from your
        ways,
    and harden our hearts so that we do not fear
        you?
—Isaiah 63:16b–17a

Isaiah recognizes the special relationship the people of Israel have with God. God is a father and a redeemer to them. God saves his people from their problems, even the problems they have created for themselves.

It sounds as if Isaiah is blaming God for when his people wander away from him, but his question is rhetorical. God is a father and a redeemer and so good to us, and yet we wander away from him. We walk away from his presence. Here, Isaiah acknowledges the problem of free will.

God allows his people, allows us, to wander from him. God allows us to harden our hearts so that we become indifferent to his presence. This is not God's will, but he allows it. Isaiah sees clearly the repercussions of ignoring God. It has led to disaster and the multiplication of all kinds of societal problems for the Israelites.

....

Are you wandering away from God in some way? Are you hardening your heart to something he wants to tell you? If so, acknowledge it and return to him. Invite him into your heart now. Thank your heavenly Father that he wants to be with you.

Tuesday, December 8
Solemnity of the
Immaculate Conception

You, LORD, are our father,
  our redeemer you are named from of old.
Too long have we been like those you do not rule,
  on whom your name is not invoked.
—Isaiah 63:16b, 19a

Isaiah recognizes the root problem of the nation of Israel: they have acted like atheists, like people who do not know God. They have not allowed God to rule over their lives and guide their behavior. Now that they have lived apart from God, they struggle to go back to him. Their sin has colored their perception of God.

When we sin, we darken our perception of God's presence. Do you notice that when you sin against someone, you are uncomfortable in their presence? For example, there is that awkward occasion of talking about someone, maybe gossiping about them, and then they walk into the room. The last thing you wanted was their presence.

This is what it is like with God. When we are sinning against God we do not want his presence. The book of Genesis tells us that after Adam and Eve sinned, they hid from God. The Immaculate Conception of Mary, the new Eve, begins the work of restoring us to his presence.

....

Pray through the intercession of Mary that you will know the joy of God's presence this Christmas.

Wednesday, December 9

Why do you make us wander, LORD, from your
ways,
and harden our hearts so that we do not fear
you? . . .
Oh that you would rend the heavens and come
down,
with the mountains quaking before you.
—Isaiah 63:17a, 19b

The people are running from God, so Isaiah cries out to God to make his presence known, to come down and be with his people, rending the veil that separates heaven from earth.

Christmas is the partial fulfillment of this prayer. At Christmas God ripped open the heavens and sent his Son into the world. But he did so quietly. It was a silent night. No one noticed that God had made his physical presence known in a little baby.

Christmas is the partial fulfillment of this prayer because it is not until Jesus' death that it is completely fulfilled. After Jesus died on the Cross, the veil of the Temple's Holy of Holies, which represented our distance from God, was torn in two. Jesus' birth, life, death, and resurrection mean that God is always with us.

....

Pray that your celebration of Christmas this year may daily draw you closer to the living Lord.

Thursday, December 10

For I long to see you, that I may impart to you some spiritual gift so that you may be strengthened, that is, that you and I may be mutually encouraged by one another's faith, yours and mine.

—Romans 1:11–12

Christmas reminds us that God gave the gift of himself, the gift of his presence. Even though his people had ignored God over and over again, God came to earth in the person of Jesus Christ.

God generously gave himself. Our first job as Christ's followers is to accept and appreciate the gift of God's presence.

Our second job is to give the gift of our presence to others. Paul tells the Romans that he longs to see them and be with them. Being in their presence is valuable to him. Your presence is perhaps the best gift you can give to people. It is a gift that no one else can give. It is an incredibly precious gift because your presence is limited to one place.

When you are making decisions about your commitments this Christmas and throughout your life, ask "Who will most value my presence?" Give the gift of your presence first of all to people who value it the most.

....

Ask the Holy Spirit to show you who values your presence the most. Pray for the grace to be present with people who most value your presence.

Friday, December 11

Then the king will say to those on his right, "Come, you who are blessed by my Father. Inherit the kingdom prepared for you from the foundation of the world. For I was hungry and you gave me food, I was thirsty and you gave me drink, a stranger and you welcomed me, naked and you clothed me, ill and you cared for me, in prison and you visited me."

—Matthew 25:34–36

When Jesus described the corporal works of mercy in this passage, two of them were about giving the gift of presence to people who were burdened and alone. He said, "I was sick and you cared for me" and "I was imprisoned and you visited me."

Your presence is a valuable gift to people because it demonstrates support for them. Look to give the gift of your presence when people need your support in facing a challenge or difficulty. Maybe you know people this Christmas who will be going through a tough time because it is the first one they will face without a spouse, child, or another family member. Support them with the gift of your presence.

....

Your presence is a valuable gift because it relieves people's loneliness. There are people who are lonely because they live alone or feel alone. Your presence can help relieve that loneliness. Who are people you know who are imprisoned, feel imprisoned, or are in an assisted care facility who you should go visit? Ask God for the grace to know who they are and to set aside a time to visit.

Saturday, December 12

Psalm 80:2ac, 3b, 15–16, 18–19

Lord, make us turn to you; let us see your face and we shall be saved.

O shepherd of Israel, hearken,
From your throne upon the cherubim, shine forth.
Rouse your power.

Lord, make us turn to you; let us see your face and we shall be saved.

Once again, O LORD of hosts,
    look down from heaven, and see;
Take care of this vine,
    and protect what your right hand has planted
    the son of man whom you yourself made
        strong.

Lord, make us turn to you; let us see your face and we shall be saved.

May your help be with the man of your right hand,
    with the son of man whom you yourself made
        strong.
Then we will no more withdraw from you;
    give us new life, and we will call upon your
        name.

Lord, make us turn to you; let us see your face and we shall be saved.

Third Week

OF ADVENT

Sunday, December 13

Comfort, give comfort to my people, says your God.

—Isaiah 40:1

God tells the prophet Isaiah to give comfort to his people. The Israelites were living in exile in Babylon, far away from their homeland and in great distress. Being separated from their home, they felt far from God as well. But the prophet assures them that they can take comfort because their situation is about to change for the better. We receive comfort when someone recognizes our problem or difficulty and tells us that we do not have to face that challenge all on our own and that they will be with us.

Today, ask God to show you how you can give comfort to his people. Pray today for the grace to be generous and to grow as a giver.

Monday, December 14

Like a shepherd he feeds his flock;
   in his arms he gathers the lambs,
Carrying them in his bosom,
   leading the ewes with care.

—Isaiah 40:11

Shepherds are often mentioned in the Bible and convey the image of an intimate and deep relationship between the shepherd and his flock. In his 2013 Chrism Mass, Pope Francis urged his bishops and priests to be shepherds living with the smell of their sheep and to reach out to those who live on the outskirts of existence. A good shepherd knows all of his sheep by name, and they come when he calls them.

Use this season to think about the sheep around you who live in the margins. Be prepared to meet them, give them comfort, and be generous to them, just like our Good Shepherd, Jesus Christ.

....

Today, ask God to give you the compassion to give and reach out to those who live in the outskirts of existence.

Tuesday, December 15

Whoever has two tunics should share with the person who has none. And whoever has food should do likewise.

—Luke 3:11

Jesus wants you to become the most generous person in your sphere of influence. He wants you to astonish people with your generosity. He wants generosity to reach into every area of your life so that, through you, he can love and intrigue the people around you. Christianity thrived in the times of the early Church because the generosity of the first Christians intrigued people. Christian generosity is radical, especially when lived out in contrast to a harsh climate of self-interest and consumerism.

Generosity is incredibly attractive, and yet it can be as simple as sharing your extras, sharing when you have two or more of something. Astonish the people who cross your path with your generosity. It is the best and most practical way to bring Christianity to life.

....

Ask Jesus to liberate you from any inclination to be stingy and to help you notice the people in need around you and open your heart and hands for them.

Wednesday, December 16

But a Samaritan traveler who came upon him was moved with compassion at the sight. He approached the victim, poured oil and wine over his wounds and bandaged them. Then he lifted him up on his own animal, took him to an inn and cared for him. The next day he took out two silver coins and gave them to the innkeeper with the instruction, "Take care of him. If you spend more than what I have given you, I shall repay you on my way back."
—Luke 10:33–35

The parable of the good Samaritan is very well known, but it needs to be reread continually. Jesus has just been challenged to explain to his listeners who our "neighbor" is. In the parable, both the priest and the Levite do not stop for the man who fell victim to robbers and was left half-dead. The expected models of religious love and charity pass him by. Maybe they were too busy and burdened with their everyday lives, but faith without works is useless and even contradictory.

The Samaritan, the pagan, knows better; he considers the person in need his neighbor, renders first aid, and then takes the injured man to an inn where he can recover from his wounds. Like the Samaritan, we are to be open to the needs of the people God puts in our path.

....

Ask God to help you see and treat everyone as your neighbor.

Thursday, December 17

Then [Jesus] said to the host who invited him, . . .
"When you hold a banquet, invite the poor, the crip-
pled, the lame, the blind; blessed indeed will you
be because of their inability to repay you. For you
will be repaid at the resurrection of the righteous."
—Luke 14:12, 13–14

Jesus has always focused on the downtrodden,
the oppressed and afflicted, the forgotten and the
neglected. They cannot repay what we do for them,
but because they cannot repay us, God will. Many
people testify that serving or giving to the poor
has changed their lives and that they have received
a lot more than they have given. Pope Francis says
that he wants a "Church which is poor and for the
poor. They have much to teach us. . . . We need to
let ourselves be evangelized by them. . . . We are
called to find Christ in them, to lend our voice to
their causes, but also to be their friends, to listen
to them, to speak for them and to embrace the
mysterious wisdom which God wishes to share
with us through them."

Quite often, the poor do not expect us to do
great things for them. They are content if we simply acknowledge their presence and their dignity,
show that we care, and share a friendly word with
them.

....

How can you be evangelized to by the poorest of your
brothers and sisters? Let God encounter you in and
through them.

Friday, December 18

Give us today our daily bread.

—Matthew 6:11

Whenever we pray the Lord's Prayer, also known as the Our Father, the only prayer that Jesus himself taught us, we come across this line. Bread was a staple food in Jesus' time, and today we still speak of the "breadwinner" in the family. Note that Jesus says, "Give us today *our* daily bread." He does not say, "Give me *my* daily bread." The pronoun "our" is an obligation, a responsibility. It reminds us to pray for food for the whole family of God, including our brothers and sisters in poverty.

God has given us extra resources not to hoard or to spend frivolously but to provide for others in need. Use this time to evaluate how you can use your extras to provide food and education and other basic necessities to those in need.

....

God has given us enough resources for everyone, but it is our task to distribute them fairly. Ask him today to help you be generous and grow as a giver.

Saturday, December 19

Psalm 33:2–3, 11–12, 20–21

Exult, you just, in the Lord! Sing to him a new song.

Give thanks to the LORD on the harp;
    with the ten-stringed lyre chant his praises.
Sing to him a new song;
    pluck the strings skillfully, with shouts of
        gladness.

Exult, you just, in the Lord! Sing to him a new song.

But the plan of the LORD stands forever;
    the design of his heart, through all generations.
Blessed the nation whose God is the LORD,
    the people he has chosen for his own
        inheritance.

Exult, you just, in the Lord! Sing to him a new song.

Our soul waits for the LORD,
    who is our help and our shield,
For in him our hearts rejoice;
    in his holy name we trust.

Exult, you just, in the Lord! Sing to him a new song.

Fourth Week

OF ADVENT

Sunday, December 20

This is the fourth and final week of Advent. When we unwrap Christmas, we see that its core is giving. God so loved the world, he gave his only beloved Son. And Jesus so loved the world he gave his life.

This week we are looking at giving joy. Our attitude impacts other people for good or for bad. As followers of Christ, we want to bring a joyful attitude so that we represent our Savior well.

....

Pray today that during the holidays and throughout the year you can bring joy to your family, friends, and coworkers.

Monday, December 21

I have told you this so that my joy may be in you and your joy may be complete.

—John 15:11

Jesus came to give us joy. Jesus even speaks about complete, lasting joy in a world where so few things seem to last. Joy is related to gladness or happiness, but it goes beyond our emotions to a state of being. It is the result of a choice.

To be joyful you have to be intentional and embrace it. It is easy to be sullen. It can be easy to get irritated or annoyed; it is much more difficult to choose joy. But even if you go through very difficult times, you can still draw strength from the joy that comes with trusting God.

....

How can you be an ambassador for Christ's joy today?

Tuesday, December 22

Splendor and majesty go before him;
    power and rejoicing are in his holy place.
Give to the LORD, you families of nations,
    give to the Lord glory and might;
Give to the LORD the glory due his name!
                  —1 Chronicles 16:27–29

The very essence, the very strength of God is the love and joy that dwell in his holy place. However, we don't always communicate that joy and thus fail to worship him properly. Some people have walked away from Christianity precisely because it seemed to be completely opposite of joy. For them, Christianity seemed to be about rule keeping, obligations, morality, or opposing certain behaviors, but the idea of it being about joy never entered the picture.

As Christians, we should act more as thermostats than as thermometers. When you act like a thermometer, you are simply going to reflect the environment you are part of. If people are joyful, then you will be joyful too. If people complain, are in a bad mood, and become sullen, you become sullen too.

Acting like a thermostat, however, means that you set the temperature in a room, in a house, in an environment. You set the tone with your attitude. The Gospel is full of joy, and as a Christian, you need to communicate this joy through your life.

....

How can you act like a thermostat that brings joy into a room? How can you allow Jesus' joy to flow through you to others?

Wednesday, December 23

I will rejoice heartily in the LORD,
   my being exults in my God.

—Isaiah 61:10a

How do we give joy to others? We can only give to others what we have. Isaiah determines that he will rejoice and find joy in God. Again we see that joy is a choice; it is in some way a matter of the will, and we have to be intentional about finding and expressing it. However, while we need to be intentional about finding joy, we cannot produce it on our own.

Joy comes from the Lord and it comes to us from a personal, intimate relationship with him. The Greek word for joy (*chara*) shares a common root with the Greek word for grace (*charis*). This reminds us that joy is only possible by the grace of God. To get joy we must connect with the source of joy through prayer, worship, and other spiritual practices.

....

Take time today to make your relationship with God a priority. Ask God to help you radiate the joy he gives you and communicate his presence to the people you encounter.

Thursday, December 24

Let the heavens be glad and the earth rejoice;
　　let the sea and what fills it resound;
　　let the plains be joyful and all that is in them.
Then let all the trees of the forest rejoice
　　before the Lord who comes,
　　who comes to govern the earth,
To govern the world with justice
　　and the peoples with faithfulness.
　　　　　　　　　　　　　　—Psalm 96:11–13

The psalm tells us that even inanimate creation rejoices and offers praise. All of creation is joyful, beautiful, and full of meaning, even if it seems purpose-free. The whole of creation—the overflowing abundance, the attention to detail, and the many ways to interact and connect with each other—spread joy and refer to the Creator.

The joy on earth echoes God's pleasure in his creation and is the true form of worship.

....

In these final hours of Advent waiting and preparation, ask the Lord to help you to worship him through spreading the joy that you experience every day.

CHRISTMASTIME

Friday, December 25
The Nativity of the Lord

Rejoice in the Lord always. I shall say it again: rejoice! Your kindness should be known to all. The Lord is near.

—Philippians 4:4–5

The theme of joy is frequent in the letter to the Philippians. St. Paul calls his brothers and sisters from the young and successful community in Philippi his "joy and crown" (4:1).

Jesus wants complete, full joy for us. But sometimes our joy is not complete because we wander away from the source of our joy. We try to find it apart from the Lord.

When we lose our joy or fail to share a joyful attitude, our job is simply to repent or turn back to God, who is the source of our joy. The Lord is near. All it takes is to call on his name and ask for his grace and mercy. When God's joy flows through us, it will be much easier to be kind to the people in our lives.

....

This Christmas Day, how can you allow God to fill you with complete joy?

Saturday, December 26

1 Samuel 2:1, 4–5, 6–7, 8abcd
My heart exults in the Lord, my Savior.
"My heart exults in the LORD,
    my horn is exalted in my God.
I have swallowed up my enemies;
    I rejoice in my victory."
My heart exults in the Lord, my Savior.
"The bows of the mighty are broken,
    while the tottering gird on strength.
The well-fed hire themselves out for bread,
    while the hungry batten on spoil.
The barren wife bears seven sons,
    while the mother of many languishes."
My heart exults in the Lord, my Savior.
"The LORD puts to death and gives life;
    he casts down to the nether world;
    he raises up again.
The LORD makes poor and makes rich,
    he humbles, he also exalts."
My heart exults in the Lord, my Savior.
"He raises the needy from the dust;
    from the dung heap he lifts up the poor,
To seat them with nobles
    and make a glorious throne their heritage."
My heart exults in the Lord, my Savior.

Sunday, December 27

> Now there were shepherds in that region living in the fields and keeping the night watch over their flock. The angel of the Lord appeared to them and the glory of the Lord shone around them, and they were struck with great fear.
>
> —Luke 2:8–9

Shepherds are prevalent figures in biblical history. They performed an important task since lambs were sacrificial animals. But even though their service was important to the religious system, they were outcasts. They did not have many social contacts, were considered rough and unclean, and lived outside the towns and cities.

Despite being religious and social outcasts, it is to the shepherds that God chooses to make a special announcement. It is this group that first hears the core message of Christianity. It is a reminder that the Gospel is for all people and that it is the humble and lowly who are able to hear this simple message of our faith: God loves, so God gives.

....

Ask God to remind you to stay humble and open to his Word so you can meet him in all of your brothers and sisters, especially in "the least" of them.

Monday, December 28

The angel said to them, "Do not be afraid; for behold, I proclaim to you good news of great joy that will be for all the people. For today in the city of David a savior has been born for you who is Messiah and Lord. And this will be a sign for you: you will find an infant wrapped in swaddling clothes and lying in a manger."

—Luke 2:10–12

The message of the angels is both simple and beautiful: Enjoy the good news of the coming of the Messiah.

The good news is that God is a giver who loves us so much that he gave us his only beloved Son (see John 3:16). If you unwrap that infant in swaddling clothes lying in a manger, that's what you find: Jesus Christ, the Messiah, the incarnated God. This is the sign the angels speak of: God makes himself small and becomes a child; he lets us touch him and he asks for our love. No barriers, just unconditional love.

Rejoice!

....

Rejoice today, knowing that God made himself a child so that we can know him.

Tuesday, December 29

So whoever is in Christ is a new creation: the old things have passed away; behold, new things have come. And all this is from God, who has reconciled us to himself through Christ and given us the ministry of reconciliation, namely, God was reconciling the world to himself in Christ, not counting their trespasses against them and entrusting to us the message of reconciliation. So we are ambassadors for Christ, as if God were appealing through us.
—2 Corinthians 5:17–20

The Christian writer Sheldon Vanauken is attributed as saying, "The best argument against Christianity is Christians." By that he meant that Christians make it hard for others to believe when their way of life does not reflect God's unconditional love. Friedrich Nietzsche echoed that thought: "I might believe in the Redeemer if his followers looked more redeemed." In other words, a God who is said to transform should "produce" people with transformed lives. Through Christ, God gave us the ministry of reconciliation and made us his ambassadors. What an enormous gift!

....

Are there areas in your life you have yet to allow God to transform? How can you accept and show that transformation so you can be a true ambassador of his unconditional love?

Wednesday, December 30

My children, I am writing this to you so that you may not commit sin. But if anyone does sin, we have an Advocate with the Father, Jesus Christ the righteous one. He is the expiation for our sins, and not for our sins only but for those of the whole world.

—1 John 2:1–2

God sends his Son not to chastise us but to rescue us. Did you ever chase a child because she was headed out into the street toward danger and you wanted to save her? That's what God did when he sent his Son. He sent him to chase after us.

Over and over again, God must come after us because we drift into sin and away from him. The Latin word for sin is *peccatum*, and it means "to miss the mark." Jesus came to earth so that we would not miss the mark with our lives but rather live in a relationship with God.

....

Jesus is our advocate with the Father. Ask him today to help you hit the mark and become more like him.

Thursday, December 31

And the Word became flesh
    and made his dwelling among us,
    and we saw his glory,
    the glory as of the Father's only Son,
    full of grace and truth.

—John 1:14

The glory of the incarnated God is not the glory of kings and the powerful but of an infant wrapped in swaddling clothes and lying in a manger. The word "dwelling" could be translated as "tabernacle," and the term goes back to the Old Testament. Moses constructed the ark of the covenant and placed it in a tent so God dwelt among his people as they wandered in the desert. Likewise, we could say that at Christmas God stepped onto our earth, pitched his tent, and set up camp right in our midst.

Jesus is full of grace and truth. He is truth and speaks truth. He calls things as they are and does not excuse sinful behavior. He is also full of grace. He understands our nature and is always ready to welcome us back when we have missed our mark and detached ourselves from him. This is the perpetual gift of Christmas.

....

Take a moment to pray for the ability to walk in grace and truth and proclaim the Good News of Christ's coming to earth.

Friday, January 1
Solemnity of
Mary, the Holy Mother of God

And Mary said:
"My soul proclaims the greatness of the Lord;
my spirit rejoices in God my savior."
—Luke 1:46–47

Christmas is a magnifier. If things are going well in your life, Christmas tends to magnify that goodness. Unfortunately, the opposite is also true. If you are struggling, the Christmas season may make the struggle seem more intense.

Rather than focusing on yourself this Christmas, on what you have and what you are, try focusing on Christ. In the NRSV translation of Luke 1:46, Mary says her soul "magnifies the Lord." We, like Mary, are told to magnify him, to glorify him. What does that mean? Among other things, *magnify* simply means "to make bigger." What if you made God a bigger part of your life? Not just during the Christmas season but every day? Allow his goodness, his will, his grace, and his truth to change your life.

....

Pray today for your soul to magnify the Lord's presence as you reflect on the miracle of the birth of Jesus, fully man and fully God.

Saturday, January 2

Psalm 96:7–10

Let the heavens be glad and the earth rejoice!
Give to the LORD, you families of nations,
give to the LORD glory and praise;
give to the LORD the glory due his name!
Let the heavens be glad and the earth rejoice!
Bring gifts, and enter his courts;
worship the LORD in holy attire.
Tremble before him, all the earth.
Let the heavens be glad and the earth rejoice!
Say among the nations: The LORD is king.
He has made the world firm, not to be moved;
he governs the peoples with equity.
Let the heavens be glad and the earth rejoice!

Sunday, January 3
The Solemnity of
the Epiphany of the Lord

When Jesus was born in Bethlehem of Judea, in the days of King Herod, behold, magi from the east arrived in Jerusalem, saying, "Where is the new-born king of the Jews? We saw his star at its rising and have come do to him homage."

—Matthew 2:1–2

The Magi, or wise men, were from Persia, what is now modern-day Iran. They were astronomers who closely tracked the movement of heavenly bodies and claimed to read them as omens of earthly events. They served as advisors to the king in his court. At one point, they were so revered in Persia that they were considered the power behind the throne.

The Magi would have never sought out the Jewish Messiah on their own. But one day they see in the sky something quite unexpected—constellations they never would have seen before. This signals to them that someone important has been born, in this case, the king of the Jewish people. This unexpected event puts them on a journey to find the Messiah.

....

When the wise men encounter an unexpected event, it moves them to seek the Lord. Pray today for the grace to seek the Lord whenever you meet unexpected problems or challenges.

Monday, January 4

Then Herod called the magi secretly and ascertained from them the time of the star's appearance. He sent them to Bethlehem and said, "Go and search diligently for the child. When you have found him, bring me word, that I too may go and do him homage." After their audience with the king they set out. And behold, the star that they had seen as its rising preceded them, until it came and stop over the place with the child was.

—Matthew 2:7–9

Herod was greatly disturbed by the thought of the Magi looking for the newborn king of the Jews. Rather than reveal his displeasure, though, Herod quietly called together the religious leaders and asked where the Messiah was to be born. They told him in Bethlehem, and so Herod sent the Magi there to search diligently for him. The Magi leave for Bethlehem.

The Magi leave together as a group and come to the child together. They find great joy. Meanwhile, Herod does everything in secret and alone. His isolation leads to anger and frustration.

....

People who succeed in times of unexpected problems are connected to community. They do not isolate themselves from others. Pray today for the grace to connect to community and avoid the pull of isolation.

Tuesday, January 5

After their audience with the king they set out. And behold, the star that they had seen as its rising preceded them, until it came and stopped over the place where the child was. They were overjoyed at seeing the star.

—Matthew 2:9–10

The Magi set out for Bethlehem and see a star over the house of the child Jesus. In seeing the star, they are overjoyed. They are overjoyed because their long journey had come to completion when they found the child Jesus.

The goal of our lives is to meet Jesus. We meet Jesus over and over again through personal habits and disciplines and by seeking him in our circumstances. We can find the joy of meeting Jesus in the circumstances in our lives if we seek him as the Magi did.

....

Pray today for the grace to seek Jesus in your circumstances. Ask Jesus to show you what he is doing in your current circumstances. How can they draw you closer to him?

Wednesday, January 6

And on entering the house they saw the child with Mary his mother. The prostrated themselves and did him homage. Then they opened their treasures and offered him gifts of gold, frankincense, and myrrh.

—Matthew 2:11

The Magi worship and honor Jesus. They honor him by making an offering. Then God warns them in a dream not to return to Herod, so they go home a different way.

When we meet Jesus we are never the same. We can't go back to the same life we once lived. Jesus offers us a better way of life, one that is more fulfilling, meaningful, and joy-filled than what the world offers us. He offers the abundant life.

....

Pray for the grace today to get to know Jesus better so you can live a more abundant life.

Rev. Michael White and **Tom Corcoran** are coauthors of the bestselling Rebuilt Parish series, including the award-winning *Rebuilt, Tools for Rebuilding, Rebuilding Your Message, The Rebuilt Field Guide,* and *ChurchMoney.* White serves as pastor and Corcoran as pastoral associate at Church of the Nativity in the Archdiocese of Baltimore. Together, they lead the Rebuilt Parish Association. They are the hosts of the CatholicTV series, *The Rebuilt Show.* White and Corcoran have spoken at conferences and parishes throughout the United States and Canada and at diocesan gatherings and conferences in Austria, Australia, Germany, Ireland, Poland, and Switzerland. They have been guests on EWTN, CatholicTV, Salt + Light Television, and numerous Catholic radio programs.

churchnativity.com
rebuiltparish.com
rebuiltparish.podbean.com/
Facebook: churchnativity
Twitter: @churchnativity
Instagram: @churchnativity